The Egyptian Cult Of Osiris

Lewis Spence

Kessinger Publishing's Rare Reprints

Thousands of Scarce and Hard-to-Find Books
on These and other Subjects!

- Americana
- Ancient Mysteries
- Animals
- Anthropology
- Architecture
- Arts
- Astrology
- Bibliographies
- Biographies & Memoirs
- Body, Mind & Spirit
- Business & Investing
- Children & Young Adult
- Collectibles
- Comparative Religions
- Crafts & Hobbies
- Earth Sciences
- Education
- Ephemera
- Fiction
- Folklore
- Geography
- Health & Diet
- History
- Hobbies & Leisure
- Humor
- Illustrated Books
- Language & Culture
- Law
- Life Sciences
- Literature
- Medicine & Pharmacy
- Metaphysical
- Music
- Mystery & Crime
- Mythology
- Natural History
- Outdoor & Nature
- Philosophy
- Poetry
- Political Science
- Science
- Psychiatry & Psychology
- Reference
- Religion & Spiritualism
- Rhetoric
- Sacred Books
- Science Fiction
- Science & Technology
- Self-Help
- Social Sciences
- Symbolism
- Theatre & Drama
- Theology
- Travel & Explorations
- War & Military
- Women
- Yoga
- *Plus Much More!*

We kindly invite you to view our catalog list at:
http://www.kessinger.net

CHAPTER IV : THE CULT OF OSIRIS

Osiris

ONE of the principal figures in the Egyptian pantheon, and one whose elements it is most difficult to disentangle, is Osiris, or As-ar. The oldest and most simple form of the name is expressed by two hieroglyphics representing a throne and an eye. These, however, cast but little light on the meaning of the name. Even the later Egyptians themselves were ignorant of its derivation, for we find that they thought it meant ' the Strength of the Eye '— that is, the strength of the sun-god, Ra. The second syllable of the name, *ar*, may, however, be in some manner connected with Ra, as we shall see later. In dynastic times Osiris was regarded as god of the dead and the under-world. Indeed, he occupied the same position in that sphere as Ra did in the land of the living. We must also recollect that the realm of the under-world was the realm of night.

The origins of Osiris are extremely obscure. We cannot glean from the texts when or where he first began to be worshipped, but that his cult is greatly more ancient than any text is certain. The earliest dynastic centres of his worship were Abydos and Mendes. He is perhaps represented on a mace-head of Narmer found at Hieraconpolis, and on a wooden plaque of the reign of Udy-mu (Den) or Hesepti, the fifth king of the First Dynasty, who is figured as dancing before him. This shows that a centre of Osiris-worship existed at Abydos during the First Dynasty. But allusions in the Pyramid Texts give us to understand that prior to this shrines had been raised to Osiris in various parts of the Nile country. As has been outlined in the chapter on the *Book of the Dead*,

Osiris dwells peaceably in the under-world with the justified, judging the souls of the departed as they appear before him. This paradise was known as Aaru, which, it is important to note, although situated in the under-world, was originally thought to be in the sky.

Osiris is usually figured as wrapped in mummy bandages and wearing the white cone-shaped crown of the South, yet Dr. Budge says of him : " Everything which the texts of all periods record concerning him goes to show that he was an indigenous god of North-east Africa, and that his home and origin were possibly Libyan." In any case, we may take it that Osiris was genuinely African in origin, and that he was indigenous to the soil of the Dark Continent. Brugsch and Sir Gaston Maspero both regarded him as a water-god,[1] and thought that he represented the creative and nutritive powers of the Nile stream in general, and of the inundation in particular. This theory is agreed to by Dr. Budge, but if Osiris is a god of the Nile alone, why import him from the Libyan desert, which boasts of no rivers ? River-gods do not as a rule emanate from regions of sand. Before proceeding further it will be well to relate the myth of Osiris.

The Myth of Osiris

Plutarch is our principal authority for the legend of Osiris. A complete version of the tale is not to be found in Egyptian texts, though these confirm the accounts given by the Greek writers. The following is a brief account of the myth as it is related in Plutarch's *De Iside et Osiride* :

Rhea (the Egyptian Nut, the sky-goddess) was the

[1] See *Zeitschrift für Aeg. Sprache*, li. p. 127 : " The Cult of the Drowned in Egypt."

Osiris   64

wife of Helios (Ra). She was, however, beloved by Kronos (Geb), whose affection she returned. When Ra discovered his wife's infidelity he was wrathful indeed, and pronounced a curse upon her, saying that her child should not be born in any month or in any year. Now the curse of Ra the mighty could not be turned aside, for Ra was the chief of all the gods. In her distress Nut called upon the god Thoth (the Greek Hermes), who also loved her. Thoth knew that the curse of Ra must be fulfilled, yet by a very cunning stratagem he found a way out of the difficulty. He went to Silene, the moon-goddess, whose light rivalled that of the sun himself, and challenged her[1] to a game of tables. The stakes on both sides were high, but Silene staked some of her light, the seventieth part of each of her illuminations, and lost. Thus it came about that her light wanes and dwindles at certain periods, so that she is no longer the rival of the sun. From the light which he had won from the moon-goddess Thoth made five days which he added to the year (at that time consisting of three hundred and sixty days) in such wise that they belonged neither to the preceding nor to the following year, nor to any month. On these five days Nut was delivered of her five children. Osiris was born on the first day, Horus on the second, Set on the third, Isis on the fourth, and Nephthys on the fifth.[2] On the birth of Osiris a loud voice was heard throughout all the world saying, " The lord of all the earth is born ! " A slightly different tradition relates that a certain man named Pamyles, carrying water from the temple of Ra at Thebes, heard

---

[1] The moon is always masculine in Egypt. I am here following Plutarch.—AUTHOR.

[2] Another version gives the children of Nut thus : Osiris, Isis, Set, Nephthys, and Anubis.

a voice commanding him to proclaim the birth of " the good and great king Osiris," which he straightway did. For this reason the education of the young Osiris was entrusted to Pamyles. Thus, it is said, was the festival of the Pamilia instituted.

In course of time the prophecies concerning Osiris were fulfilled, and he became a great and wise king. The land of Egypt flourished under his rule as it had never done heretofore. Like many another 'hero-god,' he set himself the task of civilizing his people, who at his coming were in a very barbarous condition, indulging in cannibalistic and other savage practices. He gave them a code of laws, taught them the arts of husbandry, and showed them the proper rites where-with to worship the gods. And when he had succeeded in establishing law and order in Egypt he betook him-self to distant lands to continue there his work of civilization. So gentle and good was he, and so pleasant were his methods of instilling knowledge into the minds of the barbarians, that they worshipped the very ground whereon he trod.

Set, the Enemy

He had one bitter enemy, however, in his brother Set, the Greek Typhon. During the absence of Osiris his wife Isis ruled the country so well that the schemes of the wicked Set to take a share in its government were not allowed to mature. But on the king's return Set fixed on a plan whereby to rid himself altogether of the king, his brother. For the accomplishment of his ends he leagued himself with Aso, the queen of Ethiopia, and seventy-two other conspirators. Then, after secretly measuring the king's body, he caused to be made a marvellous chest, richly fashioned and adorned, which would contain exactly the body of

66

Osiris beguiled into the Chest
Evelyn Paul

66

Osiris. This done, he invited his fellow-plotters and his brother the king to a great feast. Now Osiris had frequently been warned by the queen to beware of Set, but, having no evil in himself, the king feared it not in others, so he betook himself to the banquet.

When the feast was over Set had the beautiful chest brought into the banqueting-hall, and said, as though in jest, that it should belong to him whom it would fit. One after another the guests lay down in the chest, but it fitted none of them till the turn of Osiris came. Quite unsuspicious of treachery, the king laid himself down in the great receptacle. In a moment the conspirators had nailed down the lid, pouring boiling lead over it lest there should be any aperture. Then they set the coffin adrift on the Nile, at its Tanaitic mouth. These things befell, say some, in the twenty-eighth year of Osiris' life ; others say in the twenty-eighth year of his reign.

When the news reached the ears of Isis she was sore stricken, and cut off a lock of her hair and put on mourning apparel. Knowing well that the dead cannot rest till their bodies have been buried with funeral rites, she set out to find the corpse of her husband. For a long time her search went unrewarded, though she asked every man and woman she met whether they had seen the richly decorated chest. At length it occurred to her to inquire of some children who played by the Nile, and, as it chanced, they were able to tell her that the chest had been brought to the Tanaitic mouth of the Nile by Set and his accomplices. From that time children were regarded by the Egyptians as having some special faculty of divination.

The Tamarisk-tree

By and by the queen gained information of a more exact kind through the agency of demons, by whom she was informed that the chest had been cast up on the shore of Byblos, and flung by the waves into a tamarisk-bush, which had shot up miraculously into a magnificent tree, enclosing the coffin of Osiris in its trunk. The king of that country, Melcarthus by name, was astonished at the height and beauty of the tree, and had it cut down and a pillar made from its trunk wherewith to support the roof of his palace. Within this pillar, therefore, was hidden the chest containing the body of Osiris. Isis hastened with all speed to Byblos, where she seated herself by the side of a fountain. To none of those who approached her would she vouchsafe a word, saving only to the queen's maidens, and these she addressed very graciously, braiding their hair and perfuming them with her breath, more fragrant than the odour of flowers. When the maidens returned to the palace the queen inquired how it came that their hair and clothes were so delightfully perfumed, whereupon they related their encounter with the beautiful stranger. Queen Astarte, or Athenais, bade that she be conducted to the palace, welcomed her graciously, and appointed her nurse to one of the young princes.

The Grief of Isis

Isis fed the boy by giving him her] finger to suck. Every night, when all had retired to rest, she would pile great logs on the fire and thrust the child among them, and, changing herself into a swallow, would twitter mournful lamentations for her dead husband. Rumours of these strange practices were brought by

Isis and the Baby Prince

Evelyn Paul   68

the queen's maidens to the ears of their mistress, who
determined to see for herself whether or not there was
any truth in them. So she concealed herself in the
great hall, and when night came sure enough Isis
barred the doors and piled logs on the fire, thrusting
the child among the glowing wood. The queen rushed
forward with a loud cry and rescued her boy from the
flames. The goddess reproved her sternly, declaring
that by her action she had deprived the young prince
of immortality. Then Isis revealed her identity to the
awe-stricken Athenais and told her story, begging that
the pillar which supported the roof might be given to
her. When her request had been granted she cut open
the tree, took out the coffin containing the body of
Osiris, and mourned so loudly over it that one of the
young princes died of terror. Then she took the chest
by sea to Egypt, being accompanied on the journey by
the elder son of King Melcarthus. The child's ultimate
fate is variously recounted by several conflicting tradi-
tions. The tree which had held the body of the god
was long preserved and worshipped at Byblos.

Arrived in Egypt, Isis opened the chest and wept
long and sorely over the remains of her royal husband.
But now she bethought herself of her son Harpocrates,
or Horus the Child, whom she had left in Buto, and
leaving the chest in a secret place, she set off to search
for him. Meanwhile Set, while hunting by the light
of the moon, discovered the richly adorned coffin and
in his rage rent the body into fourteen pieces, which he
scattered here and there throughout the country.

Upon learning of this fresh outrage on the body of
the god, Isis took a boat of papyrus-reeds and journeyed
forth once more in search of her husband's remains.
After this crocodiles would not touch a papyrus
boat, probably because they thought it contained the

goddess, still pursuing her weary search. Whenever Isis found a portion of the corpse she buried it and built a shrine to mark the spot. It is for this reason that there are so many tombs of Osiris in Egypt.[1]

The Vengeance of Horus

By this time Horus had reached manhood, and Osiris, returning from the Duat, where he reigned as king of the dead, encouraged him to avenge the wrongs of his parents. Horus thereupon did battle with Set, the victory falling now to one, now to the other. At one time Set was taken captive by his enemy and given into the custody of Isis, but the latter, to her son's amazement and indignation, set him at liberty. So angry was Horus that he tore the crown from his mother's head. Thoth, however, gave her a helmet in the shape of a cow's head. Another version states that Horus cut off his mother's head, which Thoth, the maker of magic, stuck on again in the form of a cow's.

Horus and Set, it is said, still do battle with one another, yet victory has fallen to neither. When Horus shall have vanquished his enemy, Osiris will return to earth and reign once more as king in Egypt.

Sir J. G. Frazer on Osiris

From the particulars of this myth Sir J. G. Frazer has argued[2] that Osiris was "one of those personifications of vegetation whose annual death and resurrection have been celebrated in so many lands"—that he was a god of vegetation analogous to Adonis and Attis.

"The general similarity of the myth and ritual of

[1] Lang states (art. "Mythology" in *Encyclopædia Britannica*) that "the Osirian myth originated in the same sort of fancy as the Pacullic story of the dismembered beaver out of whose body things were made." [2] *Golden Bough*, vol. ii. p. 137.

The Departure of Isis from Byblos

Evelyn Paul

70

Osiris to those of Adonis and Attis," says Sir J. G. Frazer, "is obvious. In all three cases we see a god whose untimely and violent death is mourned by a loving goddess and annually celebrated by his worshippers. The character of Osiris as a deity of vegetation is brought out by the legend that he was the first to teach men the use of corn, and by the custom of beginning his annual festival with the tillage of the ground. He is said also to have introduced the cultivation of the vine. In one of the chambers dedicated to Osiris in the great temple of Isis at Philæ the dead body of Osiris is represented with stalks of corn springing from it, and a priest is depicted watering the stalks from a pitcher which he holds in his hand. The accompanying legend sets forth that 'this is the form of him whom one may not name, Osiris of the mysteries, who springs from the returning waters.' It would seem impossible to devise a more graphic way of depicting Osiris as a personification of the corn ; while the inscription attached to the picture proves that this personification was the kernel of the mysteries of the god, the innermost secret that was only revealed to the initiated. In estimating the mythical character of Osiris, very great weight must be given to this monument. The story that his mangled remains were scattered up and down the land may be a mythical way of expressing either the sowing or the winnowing of the grain. The latter interpretation is supported by the tale that Isis placed the severed limbs of Osiris on a corn-sieve. Or the legend may be a reminiscence of the custom of slaying a human victim as a representative of the corn-spirit, and distributing his flesh or scattering his ashes over the fields to fertilize them.

"But Osiris was more than a spirit of the corn ; he was also a tree-spirit, and this may well have been his

original character, since the worship of trees is naturally
older in the history of religion than the worship of the
cereals. His character as a tree-spirit was represented
very graphically in a ceremony described by Firmicus
Maternus. A pine-tree having been cut down, the
centre was hollowed out, and with the wood thus exca-
vated an image of Osiris was made, which was then
'buried' in the hollow of the tree. Here, again, it is
hard to imagine how the conception of a tree as tenanted
by a personal being could be more plainly expressed.
The image of Osiris thus made was kept for a year
and then burned, exactly as was done with the image of
Attis which was attached to the pine-tree. The ceremony of cutting the tree, as described by Firmicus
Maternus, appears to be alluded to by Plutarch. It
was probably the ritual counterpart of the mythical
discovery of the body of Osiris enclosed in the erica-
tree. We may conjecture that the erection of the *Tatu*
pillar at the close of the annual festival of Osiris was
identical with the ceremony described by Firmicus ; it
is to be noted that in the myth the erica-tree formed a
pillar in the king's house. Like the similar custom of
cutting a pine-tree and fastening an image to it, in the
rites of Attis, the ceremony perhaps belonged to the
class of customs of which the bringing in the Maypole
is among the most familiar. As to the pine-tree in
particular, at Denderah the tree of Osiris is a conifer,
and the coffer containing the body of Osiris is here
depicted as enclosed within the tree. A pine-cone often
appears on the monuments as an offering presented to
Osiris, and a manuscript of the Louvre speaks of the
cedar as sprung from him. The sycamore and the
tamarisk are also his trees. In inscriptions he is spoken
of as residing in them, and his mother Nut is frequently
portrayed in a sycamore. In a sepulchre at How

72

(Diospolis Parva) a tamarisk is depicted overshadowing the coffer of Osiris; and in the series of sculptures which illustrate the mystic history of Osiris in the great temple of Isis at Philæ a tamarisk is figured with two men pouring water on it. The inscription on this last monument leaves no doubt, says Brugsch, that the verdure of the earth was believed to be connected with the verdure of the tree, and that the sculpture refers to the grave of Osiris at Philæ, of which Plutarch tells us that it was overshadowed by a *methide* plant, taller than any olive-tree. This sculpture, it may be observed, occurs in the same chamber in which the god is depicted as a corpse with ears of corn sprouting from him. In inscriptions he is referred to as 'the one in the tree,' 'the solitary one in the acacia,' and so forth. On the monuments he sometimes appears as a mummy covered with a tree or with plants. It accords with the character of Osiris as a tree-spirit that his worshippers were forbidden to injure fruit-trees, and with his character as a god of vegetation in general that they were not allowed to stop up wells of water, which are so important for the irrigation of hot southern lands."

Sir J. G. Frazer goes on to combat the theory of Lepsius that Osiris was to be identified with the sun-god Ra. Osiris, says the German scholar, was named Osiris-Ra even in the *Book of the Dead*, and Isis, his spouse, is often called the royal consort of Ra. This identification, Sir J. G. Frazer thinks, may have had a political significance. He admits that the myth of Osiris might express the daily appearance and disappearance of the sun, and points out that most of the writers who favour the solar theory are careful to indicate that it is the daily, and not the annual, course of the sun to which they understand the myth to apply. But, then, why, pertinently asks Sir J. G. Frazer, was it celebrated by an annual ceremony? "This fact alone seems fatal to the interpretation of the myth as descriptive of sunset and sunrise. Again, though the sun may be said to die daily, in what sense can it be said to be torn in pieces?"

Plutarch says that some of the Egyptian philosophers interpreted Osiris as the moon, "because the moon, with her humid and generative light, is favourable to the propagation of animals and the growth of plants." Among primitive peoples the moon is regarded as a great source of moisture. Vegetation is thought to flourish beneath her pale rays, and she is understood as fostering the multiplication of the human species as well as animal and plant life. Sir J. G. Frazer enumerates several reasons to prove that Osiris possessed a lunar significance. Briefly these are that he is said to have lived or reigned twenty-eight years, the mythical expression of a lunar month, and that his body is said to have been rent into fourteen pieces—" This might be interpreted as the waning moon, which appears to lose a portion of itself on each of the fourteen days that make up the second half of the lunar month." Typhon found the body of Osiris at the full moon; thus its dismemberment would begin with the waning of the moon.

Primitive Conceptions of the Moon

Primitive man explains the waning moon as actually dwindling, and it appears to him as if it is being broken in pieces or eaten away. The Klamath Indians of South-west Oregon allude to the moon as 'the One Broken in Pieces,' and the Dacotas believe that when the moon is full a horde of mice begin to nibble at one side of it until they have devoured the whole. To continue Sir J. G. Frazer's argument, he quotes Plutarch to the effect that at the new moon of the month Phanemoth, which was the beginning of spring, the Egyptians celebrated what they called 'the entry of Osiris into the moon'; that at the ceremony called the 'Burial of Osiris' they made a crescent-shaped chest, "because the moon when it approaches the sun assumes the form of a crescent and vanishes"; and that once a year, at the full moon, pigs (possibly symbolical of Set, or Typhon) were sacrificed simultaneously to the moon and to Osiris. Again, in a hymn supposed to be addressed by Isis to Osiris it is said that Thoth

> Placeth thy soul in the barque Maat
> In that name which is thine of god-moon.

And again :

> Thou who comest to us as a child each month,
> We do not cease to contemplate thee.
> Thine emanation heightens the brilliancy
> Of the stars of Orion in the firmament.

In this hymn Osiris is deliberately identified with the moon.[1]

In effect, then, Sir James Frazer's theory regarding Osiris is that he was a vegetation or corn god, who later became identified, or confounded, with the moon. But surely it is as reasonable to suppose that it was because of his status as moon-god that he ranked as a deity of vegetation.

A brief consideration of the circumstances connected with lunar worship might lead us to some such supposition. The sun in his status of deity requires but little explanation. The phenomena of growth are attributed to his agency at an early period of human thought, and it is probable that wind, rain, and other atmospheric manifestations are likewise credited to his

[1] See M. A. Murray, *Osireion at Abydos*, p. 26.

action, or regarded as emanations from him. Especially is this the case in tropical climates, where the rapidity of vegetable growth is such as to afford to man an absolute demonstration of the solar power. By analogy, then, that sun of the night, the moon, comes to be regarded as an agency of growth, and primitive peoples attribute to it powers in this respect almost equal to those of the sun. Again, it must be borne in mind that, for some reason still obscure, the moon is regarded as the great reservoir of magical power. The two great orbs of night and day require but little excuse for godhead. To primitive man the sun is obviously godlike, for upon him the barbarian agriculturist depends for his very existence, and there is behind him no history of an evolution from earlier forms. It is likewise with the moon-god. In the Libyan desert at night the moon is an object which dominates the entire landscape, and it is difficult to believe that its intense brilliance and all-pervading light must not have deeply impressed the wandering tribes of that region with a sense of reverence and worship. Indeed, reverence for such an object might well precede the worship of a mere corn and tree spirit, who in such surroundings could not have much scope for the manifestation of his powers. We can see, then, that this moon-god of the Neolithic Nubians, imported into a more fertile land, would speedily become identified with the powers of growth through moisture, and thus with the Nile itself.

Osiris in his character of god of the dead affords no great difficulties of elucidation, and in this one figure we behold the junction of the ideas of the moon, moisture, the under-world, and death—in fact, all the phenomena of birth and decay.

A Shrine of Osiris
(XIIth Dynasty)

76

OSIRIS AND THE PERSEPHONE MYTH

Osiris and the Persephone Myth

The reader cannot fail to have observed the very close resemblance between the myth of Osiris and that of Demeter and Kore, or Persephone. Indeed, some of the adventures of Isis, notably that concerning the child of the king of Byblos, are practically identical with incidents in the career of Demeter. It is highly probable that the two myths possessed a common origin. But whereas in the Greek example we find the mother searching for her child, in the Egyptian myth the wife searches for the remains of her husband. In the Greek tale we have Pluto as the husband of Persephone and the ruler of the under-world also regarded, like Osiris, as a god of grain and growth, whilst Persephone, like Isis, probably personifies the grain itself. In the Greek myth we have one male and two female principles, and in the Egyptian one male and one female. The analogy could perhaps be pressed further by the inclusion in the Egyptian version of the goddess Nephthys, who was a sister-goddess to Isis or stood to her in some such relationship. It would seem, then, as if the Hellenic myth had been sophisticated by early Egyptian influences, perhaps working through a Cretan intercommunication.

It remains, then, to regard Osiris in the light of ruler of the underworld. To some extent this has been done in the chapter which deals with the *Book of the Dead*. The god of the underworld, as has been pointed out, is in nearly every instance a god of vegetable growth, and it was not because Osiris was god of the dead that he presided over fertility, but the converse. To speak more plainly, Osiris was first god of fertility, and the circumstance that he presided over the underworld was a later innovation. But it

77

was not adventitious; it was the logical outcome of his status as god of growth.

A New Osirian Theory

We must also take into brief consideration his personification of Ra, whom he meets, blends with, and under whose name he nightly sails through his own dominions. This would seem like the fusion of a sun and moon myth; the myth of the sun travelling nightly beneath the earth fused with that of the moon's nocturnal journey across the vault of heaven. A moment's consideration will show how this fusion took place. Osiris was a moon-god. That circumstance accounts for one half of the myth; the other half is to be accounted for as follows: Ra, the sun-god, must perambulate the underworld at night if he is to appear on the fringes of the east in the morning. But Osiris as a lunar deity, and perhaps as the older god, as well as in his character as god of the underworld, is already occupying the orbit he must trace. The orbits of both deities are fused in one, and there would appear to be some proof of this in the fact that, in the realm of Seker, Afra (or Ra-Osiris) changes the direction of his journey from north to south to a line due east toward the mountains of sunrise. The fusion of the two myths is quite a logical one, as the moon during the night travels in the same direction as the sun has taken during the day—that is, from east to west.

It will readily be seen how Osiris came to be regarded not only as god and judge of the dead, but also as symbolical of the resurrection of the body of man. Sir James Frazer lays great stress upon a picture of Osiris in which his body is shown covered with sprouting shoots of corn, and he seems to be of opinion that this is positive evidence that Osiris was a corn-

78

god. In our view the picture is simply symbolical of resurrection. The circumstance that Osiris is represented in the picture as in the recumbent position of the dead lends added weight to this supposition. The corn-shoot is a world-wide symbol of resurrection. In the Eleusinian mysteries a shoot of corn was shown to the neophytes as typical of physical rebirth, and a North American Indian is quoted by Loskiel, one of the Moravian Brethren, as having spoken : "We Indians shall not for ever die. Even the grains of corn we put under the earth grow up and become living things." Among the Maya of Central America, as well as among the Mexicans, the maize-goddess has a son, the young, green, tender shoot of the maize plant, who is strongly reminiscent of Horus, the son of Osiris, and who may be taken as typical of bodily resurrection. Later the vegetation myth clustering round Osiris was metamorphosed into a theological tenet regarding human resurrection, and Osiris was believed to have been once a human being who had died and had been dismembered. His body, however, was made whole again by Isis, Anubis and Horus acting upon the instructions of Thoth. A good deal of magical ceremony appears to have been mingled with the process, and this in turn was utilized in the case of every dead Egyptian by the priests in connexion with the embalmment and burial of the dead in the hope of resurrection. Osiris, however, was regarded as the principal cause of human resurrection, and he was capable of giving life after death because he had attained to it. He was entitled 'Eternity and Everlastingness,' and he it was who made men and women to be born again. This conception of resurrection appears to have been in vogue in Egypt from very early times. The great authority upon Osiris is the *Book of the Dead*, which

79

might well be called the 'Book of Osiris,' and in which are recounted his daily doings and his nightly journeyings in his kingdom of the underworld.

Isis

Isis, or Ast, must be regarded as one of the earliest and most important conceptions of female godhead in ancient Egypt. In the dynastic period she was regarded as the feminine counterpart of Osiris, and we may take it that before the dawn of Egyptian history she occupied a similar position. The philology of the name appears to be unfathomable. No other deity has probably been worshipped for such an extent of time, for her cult did not perish with that of most other Egyptian gods, but flourished later in Greece and Rome, and is seriously carried on in Paris to-day.

Isis was perhaps of Libyan origin, and is usually depicted in the form of a woman crowned with her name-symbol and holding in her hand a sceptre of papyrus. Her crown is surmounted by a pair of horns holding a disk, which in turn is sometimes crested by her hieroglyph, which represents a seat or throne. Sometimes also she is represented as possessing radiant and many-coloured wings, with which she stirs to life the inanimate body of Osiris.

No other goddess was on the whole so popular with the Egyptians, and the reason for this is probably to be found in the circumstances of travail and pity which run through her myth. These drew the sympathies of the people to her, but they were not the only reasons why she was beloved by the Egyptian masses, for she was the great and beneficent mother-goddess and represented the maternal spirit in its most intimate and affectionate guise. In her myth, perhaps one of the most touching and beautiful which ever sprang

Isis

Photo W. A. Mansell & Co.

from the consciousness of a people, we find evolved from what may have been a mere corn-spirit a type of wifely and maternal affection mourning the death of her cherished husband, and seeking by every means in her power to restore him to life.

Isis as the Wind

Although Isis had undoubtedly many forms, and although she may be regarded as the great corn-mother of Egypt, the probabilities are that in one of her phases she represents the wind of heaven. This does not appear to have been recognized by students of Egyptology, but the record seems a fairly clear one. Osiris in his guise of the corn dies and comes to life again and is sown broadcast over the land. Isis is disconsolate and moans terribly over his loss ; in fact, so loud and heartrending is her grief that the child of the King of Byblos, whom she is nursing, dies of terror. From her, grateful odours emanate, as the women of the Queen of Byblos experience. She transforms herself into a swallow. She restores the dead Osiris to life by fanning him with her wings and filling his mouth and nostrils with sweet air. It is noteworthy that she is one of the few Egyptian deities who possess wings. She is a great traveller, and unceasingly moans and sobs. If these qualities and circumstances are not allegorical of the wind, a much more ingenious hypothesis than the above will be necessary to account for their mythological connexion. Isis wails like the wind, she shrieks in tempest, she carries the fragrance of spices and flowers throughout the country, she takes the shape of a swallow, one of the swiftest of birds and typical of the rapidity of the wind, she employs the element of which she is mistress to revivify the dead Osiris, she possesses wings, as do all deities connected with the wind, and like the rest of her kind she is constantly travelling up and down the land. We do not advance the hypothesis that she is a wind-goddess *par excellence*, but in one of her phases she certainly typifies the revivifying power of the spring wind, which wails and sobs over the grave of the sleeping grain, bringing reanimating breath to the inert seeds.

Isis is one of those deities who from fortuitous and other circumstances are fated to achieve greatness. From a Libyan spirit connected in some manner with the growth of the crops, she rose to such supreme importance during her reign of nearly four thousand years in Egypt that every description of attribute was heaped upon her in abundance. This is invariably the case with successful deities. Not only do they absorb the attributes of their contemporaries in the pantheon, but qualities which are actually at variance with their original character are grafted upon them because of their very popularity. This was the case, for instance, with Tezcatlipoca, a Mexican deity, originally god of the air, who later became god of fate and fortune, and practically head of the Aztec pantheon ; and many other instances might be adduced. Thus Isis is a giver of life and food to the dead in the Duat—that is, she brings with her the fresh air of heaven into the underworld—and as the air-god Tezcatlipoca was identified with justice, so Isis is identified with Maāt, the goddess of justice.

Isis may also typify the wind of morning, from which the sun is born. In most countries at the moment of sunrise a wind springs up which may be said to usher the sun into existence. In her myth, too, we find that on leaving the house where she had been imprisoned by Set (the summer dwelling of the

Winged Isis

82

(The wings are in the attitude of protecting Horus)

Photo W. A. Mansell & Co.

wind, which during that season leaves Egypt altogether) she is preceded by seven scorpions, the fierce-stinging blasts of winter. They show her the way through swamps and marshes. Women shut the doors in her face; a child is stung by one of the scorpions, but Isis restores it to life—that is, the child recovers with the approach of better weather. Her own son Horus is stung by a scorpion—that is, the heat of the sun is rendered weak by the cold of winter until it is restored by Isis, the genial spring wind.

Manifold Attributes of Isis

The myth of Isis became so real to the people of Egypt that they came to regard her very intimately indeed, and fully believed that she had once been a veritable woman. In a more allegorical manner she was of course the great feminine fructifier of the soil. She was also a powerful enchantress, as is shown by the number of deities and human beings whom she rescued from death. Words of great and compelling power were hers. Her astronomical symbol was the star Sept, which marked the spring and the approach of the inundation of the Nile, an added evidence that in one of her phases she was goddess of the winds of spring. As the light-giver at this season of the year she was called Khut, and as goddess of the fruitful earth Usert. As the force which impelled the powers of spring and sent forth the Nile flood she was Sati, and as the goddess of fertile waters she was Anqet. She was further the deity of cultivated lands and fields, goddess of harvest and goddess of food. So that from first to last she personified the forces which make for growth and nourishment. She personifies the power of the spring season, the power of the earth to grow and yield grain, motherhood and all the attributes and

83

affinities which spring therefrom. It is not necessary in this place to trace her worship into Greece, Rome, and Western Europe, where it became greatly degraded from its pristine purity. The dignified worship of the great mother took on under European auspices an orgiastic character which appealed to the false mystic of Greece, Rome, Gaul, and Britain just as it does to-day to his Transatlantic or Parisian prototype. But the strength of the cult in the country of its origin is evinced by the circumstance that it was not finally deserted until the middle of the fifth century A.D.

Horus

As we have seen, the god Ra was depicted as a falcon, but there was another god of similar form who had been worshipped before him in the land of Egypt. This was the god Heru, or Horus, 'He who is above.' This god had many shapes. As Horus the Elder he is delineated as a man with the head of a falcon, and was believed to be the son of Geb and Nut. Horus proper was perhaps regarded as the face of heaven, the countenance of the sky, and as Horus the Elder he represented the face by day in contradistinction to Set, who was the face by night. Horus the Younger, or Harpocrates as he was called by the Greeks to distinguish him from Horus the Elder, is represented as a youth, and was the son of a Horus-god and the goddess Rat-Tauit, who appears to have been worshipped at Hermonthis in the form of a hippopotamus. Horus the Younger represented the earliest rays of the rising sun, and had no fewer than seven aspects or forms. To detail all the variants of Horus would be foreign to the purpose of this work, so it must suffice to enumerate the more important of them. The Horus of the Two Horizons, the Harmachis of the Greeks, was one of the chief forms of the sun-god Ra, and represented the sun in his diurnal course from sunrise to sunset. He thus included the personalities of Ra, Tem, and Khepera, and this affords a good example of the widespread system of overlapping which obtained in Egyptian mythology, and which does not appear to such an extent in any other mythology. Probably a number of these Horus-gods were local. Thus we find Harmachis worshipped principally at Heliopolis and Apollinopolis. His best-known monument is the famous Sphinx, near the pyramids of Gizeh. We find the first mention of the Sphinx in inscriptions in the days of Thothmes IV, when we read in the text inscribed on the stele between the paws of the Sphinx the following legend of Thothmes and the Sphinx.

The Dream of Thothmes

There was a king in Egypt called Thothmes, a mighty monarch, skilled in the arts of war and of the chase. He was good to look upon, too, with a beauty like unto that of Horus, whom Isis bare in the Northern Marshes, and greatly was he loved by gods and men.

He was wont to hunt in the burning desert, alone, or with only a few companions, and this is told of one of his hunting expeditions.

One day, before he had ascended the throne of Egypt, he was hunting unattended in the desert. It was noontide, and the sun beat fiercely down upon him, so that he was fain to seek the shadow of the mighty Harmachis, the Sphinx. Great and powerful was the god, and very majestic was his image, with the face of a man and the body of a lion, a snake upon his brow. In many temples were sacrifices made to him, in many towns did men worship with their faces turned toward him.

In the great cool shadow Thothmes laid himself

85

down to rest, and sleep enchained his senses. And as he slept he dreamed, and behold! the Sphinx opened its lips and spoke to him; it was no longer a thing of motionless rock, but the god himself, the great Harmachis. And he addressed the dreamer thus :

"Behold me, O Thothmes, for I am the Sun-god, the ruler of all peoples. Harmachis is my name, and Ra, and Khepera, and Tem. I am thy father, and thou art my son, and through me shall all good come upon thee if thou wilt hearken to my words. The land of Egypt shall be thine, and the North Land, and the South Land. In prosperity and happiness shalt thou rule for many years."

He paused, and it seemed to Thothmes as if the god were struggling to free himself from the over-whelming sands, for only his head was visible.

"It is as thou seest," Harmachis resumed; "the sands of the desert are over me. Do that quickly which I command thee, O my son Thothmes."

Ere Thothmes could reply the vision faded and he awoke. The living god was gone, and in his place was the mighty image, hewn from the solid rock.

And here the story must perforce end. It is inscribed on a stele in the little temple which lies between the paws of the Sphinx, and the remainder of the inscription is so defaced as to be indecipherable.

Heru-Behudeti

One of the greatest and most important of all the forms of Horus is Heru-Behudeti, who typifies midday, and therefore the greatest heat of the sun. It was in this form that Horus waged war against Set. His principal shrines were at Edfû, Philæ, Mesen, Aat-ab, and Tanis, where he was worshipped under the form of a lion trampling upon its enemies. In general, however, he is depicted as hawk-headed and bearing in his hand a weapon, usually a club or mace to symbolize his character as a destroyer. In the old Arthurian romances, and, indeed, in many mediæval tales which have a mythological ancestry, we read of how certain knights in combat with their enemies grew stronger as the sun waxed in the heavens, and when his beams declined their strength failed them. So was it with Sir Belin, with King Arthur, who in his frenzy slew thousands, and with St George, the patron saint of England, originally an Egyptian hero. These figures were all probably sun-gods at some early period of their development. They are obscure in birth and origin, as is the luminary they symbolize— that is, they spring from the darkness. Arthur's origin, for example, was unknown to him until the age of manhood, and the same holds good of Beowulf. As they grew in power, like the sun which they typify, the solar heroes frequently became insane, and laid about them with such pitiless fury that they slaughtered thousands in a manner of which no ordinary paladin would be capable. This is typical of the strength and fury of the sun at midday in Eastern climates. Heru-Behudeti, then, because he was god of the midday sun, was the pitiless warrior wielding the club, perhaps typifying sunstroke, and the bow and arrows, symbolizing his fierce beams which were to destroy the dragon of night and his fiendish crew. He was well represented as a lion, for what is so fierce as the tropical sun? At midday he was all-conquering and had trampled the night-dragon out of sight. In this manner, too, he represented the force of good against that of evil. The following is the myth of his battles with Set and the battalions of his evil companions.

The Myth of the Winged Disk

In the year 363 of the reign of Ra-Horakhti upon the earth it befell that the god was in Nubia with a mighty army. Set, the Evil One, had rebelled against him, for Ra was advanced in years, and Set was of all beings the most cunning and treacherous. He it was also who had slain his twin-brother Osiris, the great and good king ; and for this reason Horus, the brother of Osiris, desired greatly to have his life.

With his chariots and horsemen and foot-soldiers Ra embarked on the Great River and came to Edfû, where Horus of Edfû joined him.

"O Ra," said Horus, "great are thine enemies, and cunningly do they conspire against thee !"

"My son," answered Ra, "arm thee and go forth against mine enemies, and slay them speedily."

Thereupon Horus sought the aid of the god Thoth, the master of all magic, by whose aid he changed himself into a great sun-disk, with resplendent wings outstretched on either side. Straight to the sun he flew, and from the heavens he looked so fiercely upon his enemies and Ra's, that they neither heard nor saw aright. Each man judged his neighbour to be a stranger, and a cry went up that the foe were upon them. Each turned his weapon against the other, the majority were slain, and the handful of survivors scattered. And Horus hovered for a while over the battle-plain, hoping to find Set, but the arch-enemy was not there; he was hiding in the North Country.

Then Horus returned to Ra, who embraced him kindly. And Horus took Ra and the goddess Astarte, and showed them the battlefield strewn with corpses.

Ra, king of the gods, said to those in his train : "Come, let us voyage to the Nile, for our enemies are

88

Cippus of Horus

83

slain." But Set still had a large following, and some of his associates he commanded to turn themselves into crocodiles and hippopotami, so that they might swallow the occupants of the divine barque and yet remain invulnerable by reason of their thick hides. Horus, however, had gathered his band of smiths, each of whom made for himself an iron lance and a chain, on which Thoth bestowed some of his ever-powerful magic. Horus also repeated the formulæ in the *Book of Slaying the Hippopotamus.* So that when the fierce animals charged up the river the god was ready for them ; many of them were pierced by the magic weapons and died, while the remainder fled. Those who fled to the south were pursued by Horus, and were at length overtaken. Another great conflict ensued, wherein the followers of Set were again vanquished. According to the desire of Ra, a shrine was raised to commemorate the victory, and his image placed therein. Yet another encounter, however, was to take place in the South Land ere the followers of Set were utterly destroyed.

The Slaughter of the Monsters

Then Horus and Ra sailed northward toward the sea in search of Set and his allies, hoping to slay all the crocodiles and hippopotami, which were the bodily forms of their foes. But the beasts kept under water, and four days had elapsed ere Horus caught sight of them. He at once attacked them, and wrought great havoc with his glittering weapons, to the delight of Ra and Thoth, who watched the conflict from the boat. A hundred and forty-two prisoners were taken on this occasion. Yet did Horus continue to pursue his enemies, always in the form of a burning disk with wings like unto the sunset, and attended by the goddesses Nekhbet and Uazet in the shape of two snakes.

Once more he overtook the allies of Set, this time at the Western Waters of Mert. On this occasion, as on the others, Horus was victorious, and nearly four hundred prisoners were brought to the boat of Ra and slain.

Then was Set very greatly incensed, and decided to come forth in person to do battle with Horus. Horrible indeed were his cries and curses when he heard the losses his army had sustained. And Horus and his followers went out to meet the army of Set, and long and furious was the battle. At length Horus took a prisoner whom he believed to be Set. The wretched being was dragged before Ra, who gave him into the hands of his captor, bidding the latter do with him what he would. Then Horus killed his prisoner, cut off his head, dragged him through the dust, and cut his body in pieces, even as Set had done to Osiris. But, after all, it was only one of Set's associates who had perished thus miserably. The Evil One himself was still at large, vowing vengeance on his enemies. In the form of a large snake he hid himself under the earth, while his followers took courage from the knowledge that he had eluded his enemy. Yet again, however, were they defeated by Horus, who slew great numbers of them. The gods remained for six days on the canal, waiting for the reappearance of the foe, but none were to be seen. Then Horus scattered abroad his followers to destroy the remnant of Set's army.

The last two battles were fought at Thalû (Zaru), and at Shaïs, in Nubia. At Thalû Horus took the form of a fierce lion, and slew a hundred and forty-two enemies. At Shaïs he appeared once more in the shape of a great shining disk with wings of splendid plumage, and with the goddesses Nekhbet and Uazet on either side of it in the shape of crowned snakes. On these occasions also Horus was victorious.

There are various endings to this myth. It is said that the prisoner whom Horus caused to be decapitated was none other than Set, whose fate, however, did not hinder him from living again and taking the form of a serpent. According to this version Horus of Edfû was accompanied by Horus the Child, son of Isis and Osiris. In the same inscription which gives an account of the battles Horus the Elder and Horus the Child are utterly confused at the end. So while Horus the Elder fights the battles, Horus the Child kills Set. They are looked upon as one and the same. On capturing Set, therefore, Horus, according to one account, delivered him into the hands of Isis, who cut off his head.

Another version, again, has it that the decisive battle has not yet been fought, and that Horus will finally destroy his enemy, when Osiris and the gods once more return to earth.

Other Horus Legends

Yet another account states that when Horus the Child had become a man Set came forth and challenged him to mortal combat. So Horus set out in a boat splendidly decorated by Isis, who also laid magic spells upon it, so that its occupant might not be overcome. Meanwhile the arch-foe of the gods had taken upon himself the shape of a huge red hippopotamus. And he caused a raging storm to break over the boats of Horus and his train, so that the waters were lashed into fury ; and had it not been that the boats were protected by magic, all would assuredly have perished. Horus, however, held on his course undismayed. He had taken the form of a youth of giant stature, and towered at the gilded prow of his boat, which shone like sunlight amid the storm and the darkness. A great harpoon was poised in his hand, such a weapon as an ordinary mortal could not lift. In the water the red hippopotamus waited for the wrecking of the boat, so that he might swallow his enemies. But this he was destined never to do, for directly he showed himself above water the mighty harpoon was launched at his head and sank into his brain. And this was the end of Set, the Evil One, the murderer of Osiris and the enemy of Ra. In honour of Horus the Conqueror hymns and triumphal choruses were sung throughout the land.

In the myth of the battles of Horus it is easy to discern what is perhaps the most universal of all mythological conceptions—the solar myth. Horus (called in the Edfû text Horbehûdti, *i.e.* Horus of Edfû) was originally a sun-god, and as such was equivalent to Ra, but in time the two gods came to be regarded as separate and distinct personages, Ra being the highest, and Horus serving him as a sort of war-captain. The winged disk, therefore, and all his train represented the powers of light, while the wicked Set and his companions symbolized darkness. Thus it is that while Horus was always victorious over his enemies, he never succeeded (according to the most widespread form of the tradition) in destroying them utterly.

When Horus had routed the enemy in the form of a winged disk, that symbol came to be regarded as an excellent protective against violence and destruction. It was therefore repeated many times—especially in the New Kingdom—in temples, on monuments, stelæ, and so on, and it was believed that the more numerous the representations of it, the more efficacious did the charm become. In its simplest form the image is

Horus in Battle

Evelyn Paul

merely that of a winged disk, but at times there is a serpent on either side of the disk, representing the goddesses Nekhbet and Uazet.

The principal version of the myth, dealing with Hor-Behûdti, or Horus of Edfû, was really a local form belonging to Edfû, though in time it gained a wider acceptance. In other forms of the legend other gods took the chief *rôle* as destroyer of the enemies of Ra.

With this legend of light and darkness came to be fused another, that which relates how Horus avenged the death of Osiris. It is noticeable that in this second myth there exists some confusion between Horus the Elder and Horus the Child, respectively brother and son of Osiris. No mention is made of Osiris in the Edfû text, but that this myth is a sequel to the legend of Osiris is implied by the circumstance that Set is handed over for punishment to Isis and Horus the Child. In the later form of the story the conflict is not properly between light and darkness, but rather between the forces of good and evil.

In this legend one of the most noteworthy circumstances is that the followers of Horus were armed with weapons of metal. His followers are called in the Egyptian text Mesniu, or Mesnitu, which in all probability signifies 'workers in metal,' or 'blacksmiths.' The worshippers of Horus of Behudet continually alluded to him as 'Lord of the Forge-city,' or Edfû, where tradition asserted he carried on the work of a blacksmith. At Edfû, indeed, the great golden disk of the sun itself had been forged, as we see from a certain inscription, and in the temple of that city was a chamber behind the sanctuary called Mesnet, or 'the foundry,' where the blacksmith caste of priests attended upon the god. From sculptures upon the walls of the temple we see that these are arrayed in short robes and a species of collar which is almost a cape, that they carry their spears head downward, and a weapon of metal resembling a dagger. Horus of Behudet, who accompanies them, is dressed in a similar fashion, and is represented as spearing a hippopotamus, round which he has wound a double chain of metal. This illustrates the story of the defeat of Set by Horus of Behudet, and we may be justified in believing that the legend possessed a more or less historic basis. Here we have a tribe or caste of metal-workers at war with what is obviously a more primitive race, whom they defeat with their weapons of metal and bind with their chains, afterward slaughtering them at leisure. It is significant that they do not slay them out of hand. For what, then, do they reserve them ? Obviously for human sacrifice. They are a caste of sun-worshippers, and human blood was as necessary to the sustenance of the sun in early Egypt as it was in ancient Mexico, where the military caste, living under the patronage of the sun, always refrained from slaying an enemy in battle if they could make him prisoner, to be sacrificed at leisure. The circumstances of the legend would appear to indicate that we are here following the adventures of some West Asiatic invader who, with followers armed with metal, landed on the soil of Egypt, made himself master of Edfû, and, marching northward, established himself in the land by force of arms. This story, or portion of history, probably became amalgamated, perhaps by priestly influence, with the legend of Horus, the god of heaven in the earliest times.

Another important form of Horus was that known as Horus, son of Isis, and of Osiris. He represented the rising sun, as did several other forms of Horus, and possessed many aspects or variants. His shrines were so numerous that at one epoch or another he was identified with all the other Horus-gods, but he chiefly represented the new sun, born daily, and he was son and successor of Osiris. He was extremely popular, as being a well-marked type of resurrection after death. As Osiris represented 'yesterday,' so Horus, his son, stood for 'to-day' in the Egyptian mind. Although some texts state that Osiris was his father, others claim this position for Ra, but the two in this instance are really one and the same and interchangeable.

Osiris became the father of Horus after he was dead; such is the origin of several sun-heroes. As has been said, the birth of such is usually peculiar and obscure. Isis, while tending the infant Horus and in fear of the persecutions of Set, took shelter in the swamps of the Delta, and hid herself and her child amidst a dense mass of papyrus plants. To the Egyptian of the Delta it would of course seem as if the sun took its rise from amidst the papyrus-covered swamps which stretched on every side to the horizon, so we may regard this part of the myth as allegory pure and simple. The circumstances of the escape of Isis from Set have already been detailed in the myth of Osiris.

The filial respect which Horus displayed for the memory of his father Osiris won him much honour from the Egyptians. He it was who fixed the details of the god's mummification, and who set the standard for the pious Egyptian son. In this respect he was regarded as a helper of the dead, and was thought to mediate between them and the judges of the Taut. In his work of caring for the deceased he had a number of helpers, known as the followers of Horus, who were regarded as gods of the cardinal points. They are given positions of great importance in the *Book of the Dead*, and shared the protection of the body

95

of the deceased, as has been mentioned in the paragraph concerning the mummy. They were four in number and were named Hapï, Tuamutef, Amset, and Qebhsennuf.

Horus, son of Isis and Osiris, was regarded as of such importance that he absorbed the attributes of all the other Horus-gods, but in certain texts he is represented as a child, with forefinger to lip, and wearing the lock of hair at the side of the head which indicates youth. In later times he was figured in a great many different fanciful forms.

The Black Hog

Ra, Set, and Horus are concerned in an Egyptian myth which attempts an explanation of eclipses of the sun and moon. Set and Horus were bitter enemies, yet Set did not dare to enter the fray openly, for he feared Horus as evil must ever fear good. So he devised subtle and underhand schemes whereby he might compass the fall of Horus, and this is how the matter fell out.

One day Horus sought Ra with a request to be allowed to read the future in his eyes. This request Ra granted willingly because of his love for Horus, the beloved of gods and men. Whilst they conversed there passed them a black hog, a huge, sinister animal, ferocious of aspect, and with eyes that glinted with cunning and cruelty. Now, though neither Ra nor Horus was aware of the fact, the black hog was Set himself, who had the power to take upon him the shape of any animal he chose.

"What an evil monster!" cried Ra, as he looked upon the animal.

Horus also turned his gaze in the direction of the black hog, in whom he still failed to recognize his

96

Nephthys

Photo W. A. Mansell & Co.

enemy. This was Set's opportunity. He shot a bolt of fire straight into the eye of the god. Horus was half crazed with the violence of the pain. " Set hath done me this evil," he cried; " he shall not go unpunished." But Set had vanished, and was not to be found anywhere. Yet for the evil that had come upon Horus Ra cursed the pig.

When the young god recovered his sight Ra gave to him the city of Pé, whereat he was much delighted; and at his smile the cloud of darkness passed away, and all the land rejoiced.

A Greek version of the myth has it that the black hog tore out the eye of Horus and swallowed it, but was forced by Ra (Helios) to restore it. The eyes of Horus are of course the sun and moon, one of which is swallowed or destroyed by the ' black hog ' during an eclipse. The restoration of light to the earth is occasioned by the joy of Horus on being presented with the city of Pé.

Nephthys

The female counterpart of Set was Nephthys. She was the daughter of Geb [1] and Nut, the sister and wife of Set, and the mother of Anubis, but whether by Osiris or Set is not clear. The words Nebt-het mean ' the lady of the house,' or sky. Although Nephthys is associated with Set, she appears to remain more faithful to her sister Isis, whom she assists to regain the scattered limbs of Osiris. She is represented in the form of a woman wearing upon her head the symbol of her name, *i.e.* a basket and a house (reading Nebt-het). She appears in some ways in the *Book of the Dead* as an assistant of her sister Isis, standing behind Osiris when the hearts of the dead are weighed,

[1] Or Seb.

and kneeling at the head of Osiris' bier. She was supposed to possess great magical powers like her sister, and resembles her in possessing many forms. She is also supposed to protect Osiris in his form of moon-god. Plutarch throws some light upon Egyptian belief concerning this goddess. He says that Anubis was the son of Osiris and Nephthys, and that Typhon or Set was first apprised of their amour by finding a garland of flowers which had been left behind him by Osiris. As Isis represents fruitfulness, so, he says, Nephthys signifies corruption. Dr. Budge, commenting upon this passage, says that it is clear that Nephthys is the personification of darkness and of all that belongs to it, and that her attributes were of a passive rather than of an active character. "She was the opposite of Isis in every respect. Isis symbolized birth, growth, development, and vigour ; but Nephthys was the type of death, decay, diminution, and immobility." The two goddesses were, however, associated inseparably with each other. "Isis, according to Plutarch, represents the part of the world which is visible, whilst Nephthys represents that which is invisible. . . . Isis and Nephthys represent respectively the things which are and the things which are yet to come into being, the beginning and the end, birth and death, and life and death. We have unfortunately no means of knowing what the primitive conception of the attributes of Nephthys was, but it is most improbable that it included any of the views on the subject which were current in Plutarch's time. Nephthys is not a goddess with well-defined characteristics, but she may, generally speaking, be described as the goddess of the death which is not eternal." Dr. Budge proceeds to say that Nephthys, although a goddess of death, was associated with the coming into existence of the life

98

which springs from death. With Isis she prepared the funeral bed of Osiris and made his mummy-wrappings. Along with Isis she guarded the corpse of Osiris. In later times the goddesses were represented by two priestesses whose hair was shaved off and who wore ram's-wool garlands upon their heads. On the arm of one was a fillet inscribed to Isis, and the other wore a like band inscribed to Nephthys.

Set

The cult of Set was of the greatest antiquity, and although in later times he was regarded as evil personified, this was not his original *rôle*. According to the priests of Heliopolis he was the son of Geb and Nut, and therefore brother of Osiris, Isis, and Nephthys, husband of the latter goddess and father of Anubis. These relationships, however, were all manufactured for him at a comparatively late period. In the Pyramid Texts we find Set acting as a friend to the dead, and he even assisted Osiris to reach heaven by means of a ladder. He is also associated with Horus and is regarded as his equal. But in time they came to be regarded as mortal enemies, who were only prevented from entirely destroying one another by the wise Thoth. Horus the Elder was the god of the sky by day, and Set the god of the sky by night. The one was in fact the direct opposite of the other.

The derivation of the name Set presents many difficulties of elucidation. The determinative of his hieroglyph is either the figure of an animal or a stone, which latter seems to symbolize the stony or desert country on either side of the Nile. As to the animal which pictorially represents him, it has by no means been identified, but various authorities have likened it to a camel and an okapi. In any case it must have been a denizen of the desert inimical to man.

As Horus was the god of the North, so was Set god of the South. Dr. Brugsch considered Set symbolized the downward motion of the sun in the lower hemisphere, thus making him the source of the destructive heat of summer. As the days began to shorten and the nights to lengthen it was thought that he stole the light from the sun-god. He was likewise instrumental in the monthly destruction of the moon. Storms, earthquakes, and eclipses and all natural phenomena which caused darkness were attributed to him, and from an ethical point of view he was the god of sin and evil.

We find the myths of the combat between Set and Horus evolving from a simple opposition of day and night into a combat between the two gods. Ra and Osiris, instead of Horus, are sometimes ranged against Set. The combat symbolized the moral idea of the victory of good over evil, and those of the dead who were justified were regarded as having overcome Set as Osiris had done. In his combat with the sun-god Set took the form of the monster serpent Apep and was accompanied by an army of lesser serpents and reptiles of every description. In later times we find him identified with Typhon. All desert animals and those which inhabited the waters were regarded as the children of Set, as were animals with red hair or skins, or even red-haired men. Such animals were often sacrificed ritually in propitiation of Set. In the month Pachons an antelope and a black pig were sacrificed to him in order to deter him from attacking the full moon, and on the great festival of Heru-Behudeti such birds and fish as were thought to be of his following

Set   100

were trodden underfoot to the cry that Ra had triumphed over his enemies.

Set had also a kingdom in the northern sky, and his peculiar abode was the Great Bear. As in some other countries, the north was considered by the Egyptians as the place of darkness, cold, and death. Thus we find that by the Mexicans and Maya the abode of the god of death was considered to be the north, and that among the latter people the hieroglyph for the north is a human bone placed before the head of the death-god. The goddess Reret, who has the head and body of a hippopotamus, was supposed to have the evil influence of Set in restraint. She is pictured as holding darkness fettered by a chain, and is considered to be a form of Isis.

It was probably about the Twenty-second Dynasty that the worship of Set began to decline, and that he took on the shape of an evil deity. The theory has been put forward that the Hyksos invaders identified him with certain of their gods, and that this sufficed to bring him into disrepute with the Egyptians.

Set and the Ass

Plutarch, in his *De Iside et Osiride*, has an interesting passage concerning the alleged resemblance between the ass and Set. He says (the translation is the old one of Squire) :

" Hence their ignominious treatment of those persons, whom from the redness of their complexions they imagine to bear a resemblance to him ; and hence likewise is derived the custom of the Coptites of throwing an Ass down a precipice ; because it is usually of this colour. Nay, the inhabitants of Busiris and Lycopolis carry their detestation of this animal so far, as never to make any use of trumpets, because of the similitude between their sound and the braying of an ass. In a word, this animal is in general regarded by them as unclean and impure, merely on account of the resemblance which they conceive it bears to Typho; and in consequence of this notion, those cakes which they offer with their sacrifices during the last two months Paüni and Phaophi, have the impression of an ass, bound, stamped upon them. For the same reason likewise, when they sacrifice to the Sun, they strictly enjoyn all those who approach to worship the God, neither to wear any gold about them, nor to give provender to any ass. It is moreover evident, say they, that even the Pythagoreans looked upon Typho to have been of the rank or order of Demons, as, according to them, 'he was produced in the even number fifty-six.' For as the power of the Triangle is expressive of the nature of Pluto, Bacchus, and Mars, the properties of the Square of Rhea, Venus, Ceres, Vesta, and Juno; of the Dodecagon of Juppiter; so, as we are informed by Eudoxus, is the figure of 56 angles expressive of the nature of Typho: as therefore all the others above-mentioned in the Pythagorean system are looked upon as so many Genii or Demons, so in like manner must this latter be regarded by them. 'Tis from this persuasion likewise of the red complexion of Typho, that the Egyptians make use of no other bullocks in their sacrifice but what are of this colour. Nay, so extremely curious are they in this respect, that if there be so much as one black or white hair in the beast, 'tis sufficient to render it improper for this service. For 'tis their opinion, that sacrifices ought not to be made of such things as are in themselves agreeable and well-pleasing to the Gods, but, on the contrary, rather of such creatures wherein the souls of wicked and unjust men have been confined during the course of their transmigration. Hence sprang that custom, which was formerly observed by them, of pronouncing a solemn curse upon the head of the beast which was to be offered in sacrifice, and afterwards of cutting it off and throwing it into the Nile, though now they dispose of it to foreigners. No bullock therefore is permitted to be offered to the Gods, which has not the seal of the Sphragistæ first stamped upon it, an order of priests peculiarly set apart for this purpose, from whence likewise they derive their name. Their impress, according to Castor, is 'a man upon his knees with his hands tied behind him and a sword pointed at his throat.' Nor is it from his colour only that they maintain a resemblance between the ass and Typho, but from the stupidity likewise and sensuality of his disposition; and agreeably to this notion, having a more particular hatred to Ochus than to any other of the Persian monarchs who reigned over them, looking upon him as an execrable and abominable wretch, they gave him the nickname of the Ass, which drew the following reply from that prince, 'But this ass shall dine upon your ox,' and accordingly he slew the Apis : this story is thus related by Dino."

In certain phases of his myth Set is symbolized as a black pig. Especially is this the case when he is shown by Ra to Horus, and tears the latter's eye out of his head.

Anubis

Anubis, or, as the Egyptians called him, An-pu, was, according to some, the son of Osiris and Nephthys, and to others the son of Set. He had the head of a jackal and the body of a man, and was evidently symbolical of the animal which prowled about the tombs of the dead. His worship was of great antiquity, and it may be that in early times he had been a totem. He was the guide of the dead in the underworld on their way to the abode of Osiris. In many mythologies a dog is the companion of the dead man to the otherworld. Its remains are found in prehistoric graves ; in both Mexico and Peru dogs were sacrificed at burial, and, indeed, the custom is a very widespread one. Now it is not improbable that Anubis may have typified the prehistoric half-domesticated jackal, or early type of dog that was supposed to guide the wanderer through the underworld. Plutarch says of Anubis that the Egyptians imagine a resemblance between him and the dog.

Anubis was particularly worshipped at Lycopolis, Abt, and elsewhere. He plays a prominent part in the *Book of the Dead*, especially in those passages which are connected with the justification and the embalming of the deceased. He it was who embalmed the body of Osiris. Indeed, he rendered great assistance to the mourning sisters, and in this he may typify the faithful and helpful qualities of the dog. This is all the more striking if he is to be accepted as the son of Set, and the whole evolution of the deity would seem to imply that whereas the semi-savage, half-domesticated dog was originally nocturnal and of doubtful value, under domestication its virtues became apparent. It is probable that, could research be pushed back to a sufficiently remote epoch, and did paintings of such an early period exist, we should find Anubis pictured as the faithful dog preceding the deceased on the journey to the Duat. Later, when every deity in the picture had received a special function through the aid of priestly ingenuity, and perhaps in an area where the jackal or dog was totemic, we find the companion of the dead still accompanying him indeed, still his guide through the darkness, but in the guise and with the attributes of a full-grown deity. How he came to be the mummifier of Osiris it would, indeed, be hard to say ; probably

Anubis

the association or the jackal with the burial-ground would account for this. He was symbolical of the grave. Professor Petrie has put it on record that the best guides to Egyptian tombs are the jackal-trails. A speech of Anubis in the *Book of the Dead*, chapter cli, is suggestive of his protective character. "I have come," he says, "to protect Osiris." In many countries the dog is dispatched with the deceased for the purpose of protecting him against various grisly enemies he may meet on the way to Hades, and it is not unlikely that Anubis played a similar part in very early times.

It is the duty of Anubis to see that the beam of the great balance wherein the heart of the deceased is weighed is in its proper position. As Thoth acts for the gods, so Anubis appears for the dead man, whom he also protects against the 'Eater of the Dead.' He also guided the souls of the dead through the underworld, being assisted in this duty by Up-uaut, another jackal-headed deity, whose name signifies 'Opener of the Ways.' These gods have sometimes been confounded with one another, but in certain texts they are separately alluded to. The name of the latter deity is significant of his probable early function. Anubis, thinks Dr. Budge, was the opener of the roads of the north, and Up-uaut of those of the south. "In fact," he says, "Anubis was the personification of the summer solstice, and Ap-uat [Up-uaut] of the winter solstice." He goes on to say that when they appear with the two Utchats, or eyes of Ra, they symbolize the four quarters of heaven and of earth, and the four seasons of the year. Plutarch has also a passage upon the astronomical significance of Anubis which seems far from clear.

At Heliopolis, Anubis was to some extent fused with Horus as regards his attributes, and in some manner he took on the character of the old fusion between Horus and Set, in this latter connexion personifying death and decay. In the *Golden Ass* of Apuleius we find that Anubis had votaries in Rome, and it is noticeable that in this account he is spoken of as having a dog's head.

Thoth

Thoth, or Tehuti, was a highly composite deity. His birth was coeval with that of Ra. Let us enumerate his attributes before we seek to disentangle his significance. He is alluded to as the counter of the stars, the measurer and enumerator of the earth, as being twice great and thrice great lord of books, scribe of the gods, and as possessing knowledge of divine speech, in which he was 'mighty.' In general he was figured in human form with the head of an ibis, but sometimes he appears in the shape of that bird. He wears upon his head the crescent moon and disk, the Atef crown, and the crowns of the North and South. In the *Book of the Dead* he is drawn as holding the writing reed and palette of the scribe, and as placing on his tablets the records of the deceased whose heart is being weighed before him. There is no reason to suppose that Thoth was totemic in character, as he belongs to the cosmogonic or nature deities, few or none of whom were of this type. Another form of Thoth is that of the dog-headed ape, which, it has been stated, symbolizes his powers of equilibrium. His principal seat of worship was Hermopolis, where Ra was supposed to have risen for the first time. To Thoth was ascribed the mental powers of Ra, and, indeed, the dicta of Ra seem to have come from his lips. He was the Divine Speech personified. But we are looking ahead. Let us discover his primitive significance

106

before we enumerate the more or less complex attributes which are heaped upon him in later times.

It is pretty clear that Thoth is originally a moon-god. He is called the 'great god' and 'lord of heaven.' Among primitive peoples the moon is the great regulator of the seasons. A lunar calendar is invariably in use prior to the introduction of the computation of time by solar revolution. The moon is thus the 'great measurer' of primitive life. Thus primitive peoples speak about the 'seed moon,' the 'deer moon,' the 'grain' or 'harvest moon,' and so on. Thoth, then, was a measurer because he was a moon-god, and conversely because of his lunar significance he was *the* measurer. As Aah-Tehuti he symbolizes the new moon, as it is from the first appearance that time is measured by primitive peoples. His eye signifies the full moon in the same manner that the eye of Ra signifies the sun at mid-day. But it also symbolizes the left eye of Ra, or the cold half of the year, when the sun's rays were not so strong. It is sometimes also called the 'black eye of Horus,' the 'white eye' being the sun. This serves to illustrate how greatly the attributes of the Egyptian deities had become confused. As he was a moon-god, so he was to some extent connected with moisture, and we find him alluded to in chapter xcv of the *Book of the Dead* as a rain and thunder god.

Thoth as Soul-Recorder

It is, however, as the recorder of souls before Osiris that Thoth was important in the eyes of the Egyptian priesthood. He held this office because of his knowledge of letters and his gift of knowing what was right or in equilibrium. Again, he had the power of imparting the manner in which words should be correctly spoken. As has already been said, the mode of speech, the tone in which words were pronounced, spelt success or failure in both prayer and magical incantations. The secret of this Thoth taught to men, and this it was that the Egyptians especially desired to learn. Through the formula of Thoth the gates of the Duat were opened to the deceased, and he was safeguarded against its terrors. The *Book of the Dead* was indeed believed to be the work of Thoth, as was the *Book oj Breathings*, a much later work.

The Greek writers upon things Egyptian imagined Thoth, whom they called Trismegistos, or Hermes the Thrice Great, as the prime source of all learning and wisdom. They ascribed to him the invention of the sciences of astronomy and astrology, mathematics, geometry, and medicine. The letters of the alphabet were also his invention, from which sprang the arts or reading and writing. According to them the 'Books of Thoth' were forty-two in number, and were divided into six classes, dealing with law and theology, the service of the gods, history, geography and writing, astronomy and astrology, religious writings and medicine. It is almost certain that most of this mass of material was the work of Alexandrian Greeks sophisticated by ancient Egyptian lore.

Maat

The goddess Maat closely resembles Thoth, and has indeed been regarded as the female counterpart of that god. She was one of the original goddesses, for when the boat of Ra rose above the waters of the primeval abyss of Nu for the first time she had her place in it beside Thoth. She is symbolized by the ostrich feather, which she either holds or which decorates her head-dress. Dr. Budge states that the reason for the

Thoth   Maāt   108

association of the ostrich feather with Maāt is unknown, as is the primitive conception which underlies her name. But it is likely that the equal-sidedness of the feather, its division into halves, rendered it a fitting symbol of balance or equilibrium. Among the Maya of Central America the feather denoted the plural number. The word, we are told, indicates "that which is straight." The name Maāt with the ancient Egyptians came to imply anything which was true, genuine, or real. Thus the goddess was the personification of law, order, and truth. She indicated the regularity with which Ra rose and set in the sky, and, assisted by Thoth, wrote down his daily course for him every day. In this capacity she is called the 'daughter of Ra' and the 'eye of Ra.' As the personification of justice her moral power was immense and inexorable. In fact, she came to be regarded as that fate from whom every man receives his deserts. She sat in a hall in the underworld to hear the confessions of the dead, the door of which was guarded by Anubis. The deceased had to satisfy forty-two assessors or judges in this hall, after which he proceeded to the presence of Osiris, whom he assured that he had 'done Maāt,' and had been purified by her.

The Book of the Dead

The *Book of the Dead*, the Egyptian title of which, *Pert em hru*, has been variously translated 'coming forth by day' and the 'manifestation day,' is a great body of religious compositions compiled for the use of the dead in the otherworld. It is probable that the name had a significance for the Egyptians which is incapable of being rendered in any modern language, and this is borne out by another of its titles—'The chapter of making perfect the Khu' (or spirit).

Texts dealing with the welfare of the dead and their life in the world beyond the grave are known to have been in use among the Egyptians as early as 4000 B.C. The oldest form of the *Book of the Dead* known to us is represented in the Pyramid Texts. With the invention of mummification a more complete funerary ritual arose, based on the hope that such ceremonies as it imposed would ensure the corpse against corruption, preserve it for ever, and introduce it to a beatified existence among the gods. Almost immediately prior to the dynastic era a great stimulus appears to have been given to the cult of Osiris throughout Egypt. He had now become the god of the dead *par excellence*, and his dogma taught that from the preserved corpse would spring a beatified astral body, the future home of the spirit of the deceased. It therefore became necessary to adopt measures of the greatest precaution for the preservation of human remains.

The generality of the texts comprised in the *Book of the Dead* are in one form or another of much greater antiquity than the period of Mena, the first historical king of Egypt. Indeed, from internal evidence it is possible to show that many of these were revised or edited long before the copies known to us were made. Even at as early a date as 3300 B.C. the professional writers who transcribed the ancient texts appear to have been so puzzled by their contents that they hardly understood their purport.[1] Dr. Budge states : " We are in any case justified in estimating the earliest form of the work to be contemporaneous with the foundation of the civilization which we call ' Egyptian ' in the valley of the Nile." [2]

---

[1] Maspero, *Recueil de Travaux*, vol. iv, p. 62.
[2] *Book of the Dead*, Papyrus of Ani, vol. i, p. 7.

A DISCOVERY

A 'Discovery' 3400 Years Old

A hieratic inscription upon the sarcophagus of Queen Khnem-nefert, wife of Mentu-hetep, a king of the Eleventh Dynasty (*c.* 2500 B.C.), states that a certain chapter of the *Book of the Dead* was discovered in the reign of Hesep-ti, the fifth king of the First Dynasty, who flourished about 4266 B.C. This sarcophagus affords us two copies of the said chapter, one immediately following the other. That as early as 2500 B.C. a chapter of the *Book of the Dead* should be referred to a date almost 2000 years before that time is astounding, and the mind reels before the idea of a tradition which, during comparatively unlettered centuries, could have conserved a religious formula almost unimpaired. Thus thirty-four centuries ago a portion of the *Book of the Dead* was regarded as extremely ancient, mysterious, and difficult of comprehension. It will be noted also that the inscription on the tomb of Queen Khnem-nefert bears out that the chapter in question was 'discovered' about 4266 B.C. If it was merely discovered at that early era, what periods of remoteness lie between that epoch and the time when it was first reduced to writing? The description of the chapter on the sarcophagus of the royal lady states that "this chapter was found in the foundations beneath the Dweller in the Hennu Boat by the foreman of the builders in the time of the king of the South and North, Hesep-ti, whose word is truth"; and the Nebseni Papyrus says that the chapter was found in the city of Khemennu or Hermopolis, on a block of alabaster, written in letters of lapis-lazuli, under the feet of the god. It also appears from the Turin Papyrus, which dates from the period of the Twenty-sixth Dynasty, that the name of the finder was Heru-ta-ta-f, the son of Cheops, who was at the time engaged in a tour of inspection of the temples. Sir Gaston Maspero is doubtful concerning the importance which should be attached to the statement regarding the chapter on the tomb of Queen Khnem-nefert, but M. Naville considers the chapter in question one of the oldest in the *Book of the Dead*.

A bas-relief of the Second Dynasty bears an inscription dedicating to the shade of a certain priest the formula of the " thousands of loaves of bread, thousands of jugs of ale," and so forth, so common in later times. We thus see that 4000 years B.C. it was regarded as a religious duty to provide offerings of meat and drink for the dead, and there seems to be good evidence, from the nature of the formula in question, that it had become fixed and ritualistic by this period. This passage would appear to justify the text on the sarcophagus of the wife of Mentu-hetep. A few centuries later, about the time of Seneferu (*c.* 3766 B.C.), the cult of the dead had expanded greatly from the architectural point of view, and larger and more imposing cenotaphs were provided for them. Victorious wars had brought much wealth to Egypt, and its inhabitants were better able to meet the very considerable expenditure entailed upon them by one of the most expensive cults known to the history of religion. In the reign of Men-kau-Ra a revision of certain parts of the text of the *Book of the Dead* appears to have been undertaken. The authority for this is the rubrics attached to certain chapters which state that they were found inscribed upon a block of alabaster in letters of lapis-lazuli in the time of that monarch.

We do not find a text comprising the *Book of the Dead* as a whole until the reign of Unas (3333 B.C.),

whose pyramid was opened in 1881 by Sir G. Maspero.
The stone walls were covered with texts extremely
difficult of decipherment, because of their archaic
character and spelling, among them many from the
Book of the Dead. Continuing his excavations at
Saqqarah, Maspero made his way into the pyramid
of Teta (3300 B.C.), in which he discovered inscriptions, some of which were identical with those in the
pyramid of Unas, so that the existence of a fully
formed *Book of the Dead* by the time of the first king
of the Sixth Dynasty was proven. Additional texts
were found in the tomb of Pepi I (3233 B.C.). From
this it will be seen that before the close of the Sixth
Dynasty five copies of a series of texts, forming the
Book of the Dead of that period, are in evidence, and,
as has been observed, there is substantial proof that its
ceremonial was in vogue in the Second, and probably
in the First, Dynasty. Its text continued to be copied
and employed until the second century of the Christian
era.

It would appear that each chapter of the *Book of
the Dead* had an independent origin, and it is probable that their inclusion and adoption into the body
of the work were spread over many centuries. It is
possible that some of the texts reflect changes in
theological opinion, but each chapter stands by itself.
It would seem, however, that there was a traditional
order in the sequence of the chapters.

The Three Recensions

There were three recensions or versions of the *Book
of the Dead*—the Heliopolitan, the Theban, and the
Saïte. The Heliopolitan Recension was edited by the
priests of the College of Anu, or On, known to the
Greeks as Heliopolis, and was based upon texts not now

recoverable. The Pyramids of Unas, Teta, and Pepi contain the original texts of this recension, which represent the theological system introduced by the priests of Ra. The essentials of the primitive Egyptian religion are, however, retained, the only modification in them being the introduction of the solar doctrine of Ra. In later times the priesthood of Ra were forced to acknowledge the supremacy of Osiris, and this theological defeat is visible in the more modern texts. Between the Sixth and Eleventh Dynasties the priests of On edited a number of fresh chapters from time to time.

The Theban Recension was much in vogue from the Eighteenth to the Twenty-second Dynasties, and was usually written upon papyri and painted upon coffins in hieroglyphs. Each chapter was preserved distinct from the others, but appears to have had no distinct place in the entire collection.

The Saïte Recension was definitely arranged at some date prior to the Twenty-sixth Dynasty, and is written upon coffins and papyri, and also in hieratic and demotic script. It continued to be employed to the end of the Ptolemaic period.

As we have previously noticed, the *Book of the Dead* was for their use from the moment when they found themselves inhabitants of the otherworld. Magic was the very mainspring of existence in that sphere, and unless a spirit was acquainted with the formulæ which compelled the respect of the various gods and demons, and even of inanimate objects, it was helpless. The region to which the dead departed the primitive Egyptians called Duat. They believed it to be formed of the body of Osiris. It was regarded as dark and gloomy, containing pits of fire and dreadful monsters which circled the earth, and was in its turn bounded by a river and a lofty chain of mountains. The part of it that was nearest to Egypt was regarded as a description of mingled desert and forest, through which the soul of the deceased might not hope to struggle unless guided by some benevolent spirit who knew the paths through this country of despair. Thick darkness covered everything, and under veil of this the hideous inhabitants of the place practised all sorts of hostility to the new-comer, unless by the use of words of power he could prove his superiority over them. But there was one delectable part in this horrid region—the Sekhet Hetepet, the Elysian fields which contained the Sekhet Aaru, or the Field of Reeds, where dwelt the god Osiris and his company. At first he had domain over this part of the Duat alone, but gradually he succeeded in extending it over the entire country of the dead, of which he was monarch. We find also a god of the Duat named Duati, but who appears to have been more a personification of the region than anything else. Now the wish of all good men was to win to the kingdom of Osiris, and to that end they made an exhaustive study of the prayers and ritual of the *Book of the Dead*, in order that they might the more easily penetrate to the region of bliss. This they might reach by two ways—by land and by water. The path by water was no whit less dreadful than that by land, the passage of the soul being barred by streams of fire and boiling water, and the banks of the rivers navigated were populous with evil spirits.

The Place of Reeds

We learn from the Theban Recension that there were seven halls or mansions in the Field of Reeds, all of which had to be passed through by the soul before it was received by the god in person. Three gods guarded the door of each hall—the doorkeeper, watchman, and questioner. It was necessary for the new-comer to address each god by his name. There were also names for the doors which must be borne in mind. The name of each god was in reality a spell consisting of a number of words. The Place of Reeds was divided into fifteen regions, each of which was presided over by a god. The first of these was called Amentet, where dwelt those souls who lived upon earth-offerings; it was ruled over by Menuqet. The second was Sekhet Aaru, the Field of Reeds proper, the walls surrounding which were formed of the stuff of which the sky is made. Here dwelt the souls, who were nine cubits high, under the rule of Ra Heru-Khuti, and this place was the centre of the kingdom of Osiris. The third was the place of the spirit-souls, a region of fire. In the fourth dwelt the terrible serpent Sati-temui, which preyed on the dead who dwelt in the Duat. The fifth region was inhabited by spirits who fed upon the shadows of the weak and helpless souls. They appear to have been a description of vampire. The remaining regions were very similar to these.

The Journey of Osiris

We find other descriptions of the Duat in the *Book of Gates* and the *Book of Him that is in the Duat*, in which is outlined the journey that the sun-god makes through the otherworld after he has set upon the earth-world. Immediately after sinking he takes the form of Osiris, which in this instance is that of a ram with a man's head. Coming to the antechamber of the Duat in the west, his entrance is heralded by songs of praise, raised by the Ape-gods, while serpents blow fire from their mouths by the light of which his Pilot-gods steer his craft. All the doors are thrown open, and the dead,

116

revived by the earthly air which Osiris carries with him, come to life again for a brief hour. All the creatures of this portion of the Duat are provided with meat and drink by command of the god. Such of the dead as dwell here are those who have failed to pass the various tests for entrance to his court, and all that they exist for is the material comfort provided for them by the brief diurnal passage of the deity. When the sun, who in this form is known as Af Ra, reaches the entrance to the second part of the Duat, which is called Urnes, the gods of the first section depart from him, and do not again behold his face until the following night. At this point the boat of Af Ra is met by the boats of Osiris and his attendant gods, and in this place also Osiris desires that the dead should receive food, light, and air. Here he grapples with the serpents Hau and Neha-her, as do most sun-gods during the time of darkness, and, having overcome them, is led into the Field of the Grain-gods, where he reposes for a while. When there he hearkens to the prayers of the living on behalf of the dead, and takes account of the offerings made by them. Continuing his journey, he traverses the twelve sections of the Duat. In some of these we see what were probably quite separate realms of the dead, such as the Realm of Seker, a god who is perhaps of greater antiquity than Osiris. In this place his boat is useless, as there is no river in the gloomy kingdom of Seker, which appears completely alien to Osiris. He therefore repeats words of awful power, which compel the gods of the place to lead him by subterranean passages from which he emerges into Amhet, where is situated a stream of boiling water. But he is not out of the kingdom of Seker until he reaches the sixth section, where dwell the dead kings of Egypt and the 'Khu' or Spirit-souls. It is at this point of his journey that Af Ra turns his face toward the east and directs his course to the Mountain of the Sunrise ; previous to this he has been journeying from the south to the north. In the seventh section he is joined by Isis and other deities, and here his path is obstructed by the wicked serpent Apep, through whose body the attendant deities drive their daggers. A company of gods tow him through the eighth section, but his vessel sails itself through the ninth, and in the tenth and eleventh he seems to pass over a series of lakes, which may represent the lagoons of the eastern delta. In the latter section his progress is lighted by a disk of light, encircled by a serpent, which rests upon the prow of the boat. The twelfth section contains the great mass of celestial waters called Nu, and here dwells Nut, the personification of the morning. Before the boat looms the great serpent Ankh-neteru, and twelve of the gods, taking hold of the tow-line, enter this serpent at the tail and draw the god in his boat through the monstrous body, bringing Af Ra out at its mouth ; but not as Af Ra, for during this passage he has been transformed into Khepera, in which shape he is towed into the sky by twelve goddesses, who lead him before Shu, the god of the atmosphere of the terrestrial world. Shu places him in the opening in the semicircular wall which forms the end of the twelfth section, and he now appears to mortal eyes as a disk of light, having discarded his mummified form, in which he traversed the Duat. His progress is followed by the acclamations of his company of gods, who fall upon and destroy his enemies and sing hymns of praise to him. The Duat, as described in the *Book of Gates*, differs considerably from that of the *Book of Him that is in the Duat*, but it also possesses twelve sections, and a similar journey is outlined in it.

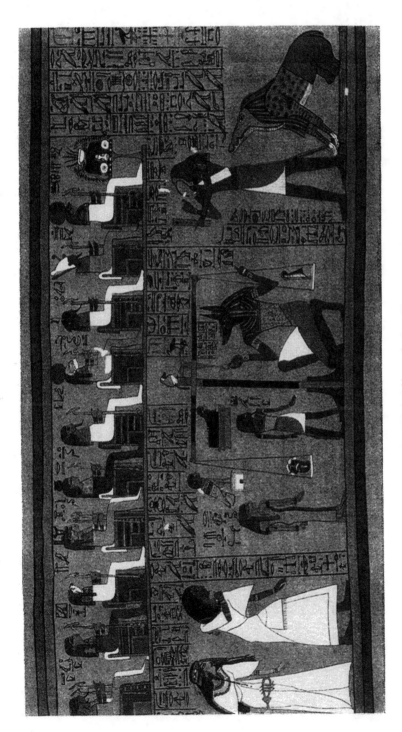

The Weighing of the Heart

From the Papyrus of Ani

THE JOURNEY OF OSIRIS

The principal gods alluded to in the *Book of the Dead* are : Tem or Atmu, Nu, Ra, Khepra, Ptah, Ptah-Seker, Khnemu, Shu, Set, Horus, Thoth, Nephthys, Anubis, Amen, and Anu—in fact, the majority of the principal divinities of Egypt. Besides these there were many lesser gods and a great company of spirits, demons, and other supernatural beings. Many of these demons were very ancient forms of half-forgotten deities. It will be noticed that at practically every stage of his journey Osiris left behind him one or more of his divine companions, who henceforth were supposed to become the rulers or satraps of the regions in which he had quitted them. So might an earthly Pharaoh reward his courtiers for services rendered.

It was only during the Middle Kingdom that the conception of Osiris as judge of the dead took definite form and received general recognition. In one of the chapters of the *Book of the Dead* we find him seated in a large hall the roof of which is covered with fire and symbols of truth. Before him are the symbol of Anubis, the four sons of Horus, and the Devourer of the West, a monster who serves as his protector. In the rear sit the forty-two judges of the dead. The deceased makes his appearance before the god and his heart is placed in a great balance to be weighed by Anubis, Thoth, the scribe of the gods, standing by to note the result upon his tablets. Having communicated this to Osiris, the dead man, if found worthy, is presented to the deity, to whom he repeats a long prayer, in which he states that he has not committed any evil. Those who could not pass the test were hurried away, and so far as is known were in danger of being devoured by a frightful monster called Beby, which awaited them outside. The justified deceased took part in the life of Osiris and the other gods, which appears to have been very much the same as that of the Egyptian aristocracy. As has been said, the deceased might also transform himself into any animal form he cared. The life of the justified dead is well outlined in an inscription on the tomb of Paheri, prince of El Kab, which is as follows : " Thou goest in and out with a glad heart, and with the rewards of the gods. . . . Thou becomest a living soul ; thou hast power over bread, water, and air. Thou changest thyself into a phœnix or a swallow, a sparrow-hawk or a heron, as thou desirest. Thou dost cross in the boat and art not hindered. Thou sailest upon the water when a flood ariseth. Thou livest anew and thy soul is not parted from thy body. Thy soul is a god together with the illuminated, and the excellent souls speak with thee. Thou art among them and (verily) receivest what is given upon earth ; thou possessest water, possessest air, hast superabundance of that which thou desirest. Thine eyes are given to thee to see, and thine ears to hear speech, thy mouth speaketh, thy legs move, thy hands and arms bestir themselves for thee, thy flesh grows, thy veins are in health, and thou feelest thyself well in all thy limbs. Thou hast thine upright heart in thy possession, and thy earlier heart belongs to thee. Thou dost mount up to heaven, and art summoned each day to the libation table of Wennofre, thou receivest the good which has been offered to him and the gifts of the Lords of the necropolis."

The *Book of the Dead* is obviously an allegory of the passage of the sun through the underworld. The sinking of the sun at nightfall would naturally arouse in primitive man thoughts as to where the luminary dwelt during the hours of gloom, for the sun was to early man a living thing. He could watch its motion across the sky, and the light and other benefits which he received from it came to make him regard it as the source of all good. It appeared plain to him that its diurnal career was cut short by the attacks of some enemy, and the logical sequel of the belief in the solar deity as a beneficent power was of course that the force hostile to him must be of evil disposition. It came to be figured as a serpent or dragon which nightly battled with the luminary and for a season prevailed. The gods of many religions have to descend into the otherworld to do battle with the forces of death and hell. We may see an analogy to the *Book of the Dead* in the Central American *Popol Vuh*, in which two hero-gods, the sons and nephews of the sun and the moon, descend into the dark abyss of the Maya Hades, rout its forces, and return triumphant. It has been suggested that the *Book of the Dead* was nothing more or less than the ritual of a secret brotherhood, and that the various halls mentioned in it symbolized the several stages of initiation through which the members had to pass.

It is curious that in his recent interesting book on *Mexican Archæology* Mr. T. Athol Joyce, of the British Museum, has mentioned that the court of the Maya underworld, as alluded to in the *Popol Vuh*, " seems to have been conducted on the principle of a secret society with a definite form of initiation." It is practically certain that the mysteries of Eleusis, and similar Greek initiatory ceremonies, were concerned with the life of the underworld, especially with the story of Demeter and Kore, or Ceres, and that a theatric representation of the wanderings of the mother in search of her daughter in the underworld was given in the course of the ceremonial. These Greek deities, besides being gods of the dead, were gods of agriculture—corn-gods ;

but gods of the underworld often presided over the growth of the crops, as it was believed that the grain germinated underneath the earth by their influence. For example, we find in the *Popol Vuh* that Xquiq, daughter of one of the lords of the underworld, was able to reap a field of maize in a few minutes in a spot where before there had been none. All this would seem to point to the probability that if the *Book of the Dead* did not contain an early type of initiatory ceremonial, it may have powerfully influenced the ceremonial of mysteries when they arose. The mysteries of the Cabiri, for example, are supposed to be of Egyptian origin. On the other hand, it may be possible that the *Book of the Dead* represents the ceremonial of an older prehistoric mystery, which had been forgotten by the dynastic Egyptians. Savage races all over the world possess such mysteries. The Indians of North America and the Blackfellows of Australia possess most elaborate initiatory ceremonies ; and it is quite possible that the *Book of the Dead* may preserve the ritual of Neolithic savages who practised it thousands of years prior to its connexion with the worship of Osiris.

The Place of Punishment

Although there does not appear to have been a portion of the Duat specially reserved for the wicked, they were sufficiently tormented in many ways to render their existence a punishment for any misdeeds committed during life. At one end of this region were pits of fire where grisly deities presided, superintending the destruction of the bodies of the deceased and hacking them to pieces before they were burned. Their punishment was, however, mitigated by the appearance of Ra-Osiris on his nightly journey, for as he advanced their torments ceased for the time being.

THE PLACE OF PUNISHMENT

The deities who inflicted punishment upon the damned were the enemies of Ra-Osiris—personifications of darkness, night, fog, mist, vapour, tempest, wind, and so forth, and these were destroyed daily by the fiery beams of the luminary. These were pictured in human form, and the scenes of their destruction by fire have often been mistakenly supposed to represent the burning of the souls of the doomed. This evil host was renewed with every revolution of the sun, so that a fresh phalanx of enemies appeared to attack Ra each night and morning. It was during the interval between dawn and sunrise that they were discomfited and punished. The souls of the doomed were in no wise enabled to hinder the progress of Ra, but in later times these were in some measure identified with the enemies of Ra, with whom they dwelt and whom they assisted to attack the sun-god. In the strife which ensued they were pierced by the fiery sun-rays, symbolized as darts or spears, and the knives which hacked their bodies in pieces were typical of the flames of fire emanating from the body of Ra. The lakes and pits of fire in which they were submerged typified the appearance of the eastern heavens at sunrise.

There was nothing in the Egyptian creed to justify the belief in everlasting punishment, and such a view is unsupported by the material of the texts. There is, in fact, no parallel in the Egyptian religion to the Gehenna of the Hebrews, or the Purgatory and Hell of medieval Europe. The Egyptian idea of death did not include the conception of the resurrection of a second physical body in the underworld, but, should the physical body be destroyed, they considered that the *ka* or double, the shadow and spirit of man, might also perish. It is strange, all the same, to observe that the Egyptian idea of temporary punishment after death appears to have coloured the medieval Christian conception of that state through Coptic sources. Indeed, the Coptic Christians of Egypt appear to have borrowed the idea of punishment in the Duat almost entire from their pagan ancestors or contemporaries. Amélineau cites a Coptic work in which a dead Egyptian tells how at the hour of dissolution avenging angels collected around him with knives and other weapons, which they thrust through and through him. Other spirits tore his soul from his body and, securing it to the back of a black horse, galloped off with it to Amentet. On arrival there he was first tortured in a place filled with noisome reptiles, and was then thrust into outer darkness. He fell into another pit at least two hundred feet deep, in which were assembled reptiles of every description, each having seven heads, and here he was given over to a serpent which had teeth like iron stakes. From Monday to Friday of each week this monster gnawed and tore at the doomed wretch, who rested only from this torment on Saturday and Sunday. In the circumstance that it does not posit eternal punishment, the region of torment, if so it can be named, differs from similar ideas in other mythologies; but in the essence concerning the nature of the punishment meted out, the cutting with knives, stabbing with spears, burning with fire, and so forth, it is practically at one with the underworlds of other faiths. The scenery of the Egyptian infernal regions also closely resembles that of its equivalents in other mythologies. It was not to be supposed that the Egyptians, with their elaborate precautions against bodily attack after death, should believe in eternal punishment. They may have believed in punishment for each other, but it is highly improbable that any Egyptian who had devoted any time to the study of the *Book of the Dead* believed that he himself was doomed. His whole future, according to that book, hung upon his knowledge of the words of power written therein, and surely no one with such a comparatively easy means of escape could have been so foolish as to neglect it.

The Egyptian Heaven

As has been said, the exact position of heaven does not appear to have been located, but it may be said in a general sense that the Egyptians believed it to be placed somewhere above the sky. They called it Pet, which expression they used in contradistinction to the word Nu, meaning sky. The heavens and the sky they regarded as a slab, each end of which rested on a support formed of the two mountains Bakhau and Manu, the mountains of sunrise and sunset. In primitive times heaven was conceived as consisting of two portions, the east and the west ; but later it was divided into four parts, each of which was placed under the sovereignty of a god. This region was supported by four pillars, each of which again was under the direction of a deity, and at a comparatively late period an extra pillar was added to support the middle. In one myth we find the heavens spoken of as representing a human head, the sun and moon forming the eyes, and the supports of heaven being formed by the hair. The gods of the four quarters who guarded the original pillars were those deities known as Canopic (see p. 28), or otherwise called the Children of Horus.

In heaven dwelt the great god Ra, who sat upon a metal throne, the sides of which were embossed with the faces of lions and the hoofs of bulls. His train or company surrounded him, and was in its turn encircled by the lesser companies of deities. Each of the gods who presided over the world and the Duat had also his own place in heaven. Beneath the lesser gods again came beings who might well be described as angelical. First among these were the Shemsu-heru, or followers of Horus, who waited upon the sun-god, and, if necessary, came to his protection. They were regarded as being essential to his welfare. Next came the Ashemu, the attributes of which are unknown, and after those the Henmemet, perhaps souls who were to become human beings, but their status is by no means clear. They were supposed to live upon grain and herbs. There were also beings called Utennu and Afa, regarding the characteristics of which absolutely nothing is known. Following these came an innumerable host of spirits, souls and so forth, chiefly of those who had once dwelt upon the earth, and who were known collectively as 'the living ones.' The Egyptians thought these might wander about the earth and return to heaven at certain fixed times, the idea arising probably because they wished to provide a future for the body as well as for the soul and spirit. As explained previously, the gods of heaven had their complements or doubles on earth, and man in some degree was supposed to partake of this dual nature. The Egyptian conception of heaven altered slowly throughout the centuries. An examination of the earliest records available shows that the idea of existence after death was a sort of shadowy extension of the life of this world. Such an idea is common to all primitive races. As they progressed, however, this conception became entirely changed and a more spiritual one took its place. The soul, *ba*, and the spirit, *khu*, which were usually represented as a hawk and a heron in the hieroglyphic texts, partook of heavenly food and became one with the gods, and in time became united with the glorified body or heavenly frame, so that the soul-spirit, power, shade, double, and name of the deceased were all collected in the one heavenly body known as *sahu*, which may be described as the spiritual body. It was considered to grow out of the dead body, and its existence became possible through the magic ceremonies performed and the words of power spoken by the priests during the burial service.

How the Blessed Lived

In the *Book of the Dead* it is stated that the spirits of heaven are in number 4,601,200. It has been suggested that this number was probably the Egyptian enumeration of all those human spirits who had died and had attained to heaven; but this is hardly probable, for obvious reasons. The manner in which these spirits employed their time is a little obscure. Some directed the revolutions of the heavenly bodies; others accompanied the great gods in their journey through the heavens; while still others superintended mundane affairs. They chanted eternal praises of Ra as supreme monarch of the gods, and their hymns described the wonders of his power and glory. They lived upon the rays of light which fell from the eye of Horus—that is, they were nourished upon sunlight, so that in time their bodies became wholly composed of light. According to one myth the gods themselves lived upon a species of plant called the 'plant of life,' which appears to have grown beside a great lake. But such a conception is in consonance with an almost separate theological idea to the effect that the deceased dwelt in a Paradise where luxuriant grain-fields were watered by numerous canals, and where material delights of every kind abounded. It was perhaps this place in which the 'bread of eternity' and the 'beer of eternity,' the celestial fig-tree, and other such conceptions were supposed to form the food of the dead. The blessed were supposed to be arrayed in garments similar to those which clothed the gods, but certain of them seem to have worn white linen apparel, with white sandals on their feet.

All this goes to show that the heaven of the primitive Egyptians was nothing more than an extension of terrestrial conditions, or perhaps it might be said an improvement upon them. So long as the Egyptian had the wherewithal to make bread and to brew beer, and had cleanly garments, and shelter under a homestead the ground round which was intersected with numerous canals, he considered that to be the best of all possible heavens. The crops, of course, would grow of themselves. The whole idea was quite a material one, if the life was simple but comfortable. There is nothing sophisticated about the Egyptian heaven like the Mohammedan or Christian realms of bliss ; even the manner of reaching it was primitive, the early dwellers by the Nile imagining that they could reach it by climbing on to its metal floor by way of the mountains which supported it, and their later descendants believing that a ladder was necessary for the ascent. In many tombs models of these ladders were placed so that the dead people might make use of their astral counterparts to gain the celestial regions. Even Osiris required such a ladder, and was helped to ascend it by Ra and Horus, or by Horus and Set. Many pictures of such ladders are also found in various papyri of the *Book of the Dead* which were placed in tombs. Its length was regulated by the deceased himself according to the power of the magical words he pronounced over it. The deceased by words of power was further enabled to turn himself into many bird and animal shapes. It is difficult to understand the reason for these animal transformations in Paradise, but the conception has a parallel in the idea of the Aztec warriors that when they entered the domain of the sun-god they would accompany him in his course and would descend to earth during part of his daily journey in the shape of humming-birds.

This is the end of this publication.

Any remaining blank pages are for our book binding
requirements and are blank on purpose.

To search thousands of interesting publications like this one,
please remember to visit our website at:

http://www.kessinger.net